DESIRE PATHS

Desire Paths

Andrew Martin

DESIRE PATHS
A SHOALS OF STARLINGS PRESS BOOK
ISBN: 978-1-913767-09-9

Text copyright © Andrew Martin 2021
All artwork copyright © Andrew Martin 2021

The rights of Andrew Martin to be identified as the author of this work has been asserted by Shoals of Starlings Press

All rights are reserved. No part of this book may be used or reproduced in any matter whatsoever without written permission from the author, except in the case of brief quotations embodied in critical articles or reviews.

First published in 2021

Shoals of Starlings Press logo is copyright © Andrew Martin 2020

Shoals of Starlings Press is based in Plymouth, UK

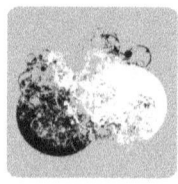
Shoals
of
Starlings
Press

i.

created as consequence
of erosion
from trails of traffic
human and animal

finding the shortest
most navigable route
between origin
and destination

width and severity
indicates how much
the heart wants
to go somewhere new
to return home

ii.

feather edged scars
across fields
through forests

etch of the river
sung into soil
through rock

the ghosts of footsteps
on their way back
out of the sea

Desire Paths

morning walk	9
is dew	10
give you the quiet	11
walking the worn edge	12
walking with you	13
river	14
if I could give you	16
I want to walk	18
sometimes you forget	19
amongst the dreaming and the dead	20
for you	22
there is a hole in a tree	23
desire threads	24
tigered	26
silver	27
dart	28
like to give you	31
diminishing	32
sometimes the world is so gentle	33

the path	34
footprints	35
envious	36
the silk circuitry	38
sea glass	40
glad	42
give you	43
holding hands	44
weight	46
standing in front of the sun	48
gloaming walk	50
promise	51
phantom paths	52

morning walk

take your hand
above dawn swept fields
walk into the dusk dusted river

we'll stretch to the sea
let half-lights wash us away
as shadows stitch us together

is   dew

the residue
of spirit bioluminescence
brushed onto grass
from the fabric of ghosts
phantom palms
faded fingers
feeling the fields
that called to them
when they had skin
to hold them back

give you the quiet

of my quietest walks
the stillness of sun
settling upon paths
sparrow shadows
flitting down their sides
before diverging
pierce your shadow
the softest of bullets

as they pass through
put back the darkness
they displace
like a thoughtful child
slowly lowering a stone
after studying
what resides
beneath its weight

walking the worn edge

I've unseen things
you believed in
doves on fire
wings shredding
in the belly of Betelgeuse
I've heard waves
shadow-shimmer in daylight
far from the desire paths
all those memories
will be found again
out of time
rain that remembers
the crying
drenched in dawn

walking with you

slowed our steps
to match our long breaths
considered the faintness
of every footfall
felt behind us
beginning to evaporate

weighed each word
in our mouths
explored their shape
with our tongues
made us speak softer

did we hear the grass
stretch skywards
as stoned sunlight
like lazy lightning
spilled its ribbons
down through leaves

your tears
tiny snails made of glass
unravelling the spiral
held in their shells
dissolving
descending
your cheek

quiet currents of air
thick as water
streamed between us

birdsong stretched
to whale song

river

rewrites the story
as it reads
its own words

braids sunlight
into the dark
of its muscle

the flame
of its brush
shadow writing

its singing
leaves scars

tugs at the tongue
unravels the fire
from an expired fox

a jug of rain water
sways a ship
within its hips

as we walk to the sea
sync our breaths
to the barely breathing waves

the river pours itself
slowly lets go
of all that it has held

the sea rolls
broken memories
fragments of faces

riddled with riverbeds
our hands remember
the water pulled through them

the rain that read us

if I could give you

my walks as a gift
I'd perforate along
all quiet paths I've taken
fold them until they'll fit
into your palms
to rest amongst
the shadow-soaked paths
already scored into your skin

take down the scaffolding
that stops our sun collapsing
compact its combustion
to a lozenge
so that dawn and dusk
can dissolve on your tongue
line your throat
with half-lights

and its honey heart
will release
the rusty bronze
and dusty silver slow worms
of sunsets and rises
into your blood
where they'll constrict and swallow
all your tiny darknesses

I'd give you the sound
of the river's thousand quills
documenting it all
in scrolls of script

and above
give you the skylark
born without a voice box
raining down its silence

I want to walk

the streets you sung
in your youth
collect the flames
flung to their sides
that still gild the gutters
with their old gold
come away with
bagfuls of autumn leaves

I'll arrange them
at the feet of reeds
listen to
the smoke skirt
of your new song
as it brushes
through their hair

sometimes you forget

there is always a river
whittling away somewhere

the sea is still
from time to time

there are paths
being quietly reaffirmed

with slow
thoughtful steps

amongst the dreaming and the dead

is love less real
because it is imagined
I imagine the tor
we would have climbed
the wind
that would have wrapped us
loosened your hair
into my eyes
tiny flares
that echoes the sun's

the crushed blues and greens
of your sea glass eyes
made brighter here
amongst the rust and ash
of the gorse and granite
surprising as a kingfisher
flashing past concrete
in a city centre
fishing in a fountain
without any fish
diving just for the joy
of breaking the surface
to be amongst the billows
of its own bubbles

here now
amongst the dreaming
and the dead
I cannot tell if

these are the places
I hope to find you now
but it is only the moors
blonde whispers
I hear calling

I did find a feather
blue as a gas flame
upon the miner's skin
of a pool of water
I deep sea dived
into its inch of darkness
in search
of your crumbled glass

to have held you
on top of the revealed
scarred heart of the mountain
to have swayed
like the bleached bone grass
beneath us

silence stretched to years
between the lub and dup
of our slowed heartbeats
blood thickened
veined with tin

the sun's slow concertina
heavy stage curtains
doused in shadows
collapsed into the pale fire
and burnt umbers
of the horizon

for you

I'd like to trace
every flight path
from a shoal
of starlings

etch their weave
into sky
reveal the desire
of the dance

from a blown candle
take its grace note
of smoke
slow its fading

so it takes
hours to thin
as it skates
in and out

of air

there is a hole in a tree

a dark flame
human sized hole
as if its heart
been hollowed out
had enough
of being a tree
became a person
walked away

if I curl inside
would this tree
take this man
tired of being a man
turn me to the soft stone
of old sunlight
let the dark lightning
of new antlers
take root into sky

or a giant moth emerged
shivered itself free
took all night
all its life
for blood to inflate
its too heavy wings
couldn't even flutter

desire threads

love your smoke
and your fire

the braided cotton
of your wick
threaded through
your candle

that curls back
into your flame
as you sing

your smoke stitched
into my dark air

the fracture
through your slate
the vein of silver
that runs through
the darkness of your silt
your silence
threaded through
my song

swallows and swifts
scratching lines
into the palms of wind
that feel the fields
between us

only when light is low
the lace revealed
our fingerprints
on each other's windows

tigered

skylark chimes the sky
blackbird skims soil
spills its throat
into footprints

ripples takes days
to finally fade
on the shores
of their sides

your darkness
would fray here
amongst the shivered
cymbals of sunlight

your shadow
would shed its coils
become something
that shimmers

slink off
dressed in stripes
fear
turned to flames

silver

want to walk
corridors of birches
to tread
slow and soft
listen to bark
unpeel
hear our scars
seal

d a r t

i.

I want to walk
with the river
take its hand
be a weave
in its weight
wake up
in its dream
where blood
and breath
thick as silt

ii.

air still
sky listening
to its slowed heartbeat
where does wind go
on evenings like these
has it hidden itself
upon the riverbed
settled to sleep
within its silt

I want to walk
into the river as well
each step unravelling me
a little more
till my tongue
tugged to a ribbon
and the tiny storms
of slate in my eyes
turn clear
in the current

iii.

silence silts my veins
thought of you
before sleep coiled me
into oblivion
saw moonlight
poured into you
even though I knew
tonight
this wouldn't be the case

tonight
a carpet of clouds
looks down upon your
sedated serpentine
the slowed churn
of your current
turning you milky
with all the souls
you sung to the sea
wind dreaming
inside you
you dreaming
inside me

like to give you

the walks
I wished I'd walked
when the river called

the spilled grain
of skylark songs
that never rained upon me

the unfrozen bracelets
of slow slow worms
I never witnessed uncurling

the dawns and dusks
that never dusted my shoulders
licked my eyelashes

the shavings
planed from the sun
that didn't soak into my skin

fold all those things
I could never give you
into your unfolded palms

diminishing

songlines
become whispers
silence etches itself
beneath skin

paths shrink
to single file
no room
to swing the lantern
our hands lit
reaching for each others

brambles
have tangled tentacles
forests
feather their edges away
scars
swallow their stitches
hidden now
beneath the fur of fields

our footsteps
froth with flowers
spark butterflies

at night
flake moths

sometimes the world is so gentle

sunset sits upon park benches
reveals old rivers
ribboning through the grain
shadows pool in a paw print
a cat whispers the piano
pads across its keys
breeze lifts the leaves a little
fingers become feathers
holding hands
a form of flight
skim long grass
filaments lit low
shadows stretch towards me
sparrows shiver cowbells
in their chests
church bells
touched by the late light
train lines sing
the miles between us

the path

I walk without you
covered
in broken glass
at its end
my scarred soles
greet the grass
as I take
the last steps
to where you wait
at the centre
of a field
roaring
with dandelions

footprints

your footsteps
soft bruises in the grass

the shadow of your weight
the weight of your shadow

already blades
peeling themselves
back into air

this is not a cold dead moon
there is wind here
that doesn't want you to stay

always desires fresh bruises

as does the tide
that panel beats our steps
back out of the shore

I'd like to walk with you
on some distant dusty moon
at the edge of the solar system

our footsteps
touched only by the dim
lamp light of the Sun

no weather
to weather them away

envious

of the wind
gets to hold all of you
all at once
feels you
within its wrists

of the sun
that brushes your hair
plays pinball
inside your eyes

of the poured shadows
that describes the shape of you
seep into your seams
collect in your shallows
flood your fingerprints

of the rain
that reads your pores
walks the paths
in your palms
retraces your tears

of the sea
that constricts your chest
squeezes the heart
it could stop

take your hand

we'll walk
into our dreams together
wander museums at night
listen to meteorites
whisper in their sleep

creep like moonlight
through fields
dust barn owls with silver
watch them sleep
with their eyes open

stars nestled
into the silt
of souls

the silk circuitry

feathers feel
the cambers
of the ceiling

wind rushes
the valley

sparks
as it slows
through the reeds

fades to a breeze
splays its sliced palms
at your feet

songs
cobwebs
etched into its fingertips
learnt the shape
of distance

returned
with the memory of melodies
smeared up its arms
down its spine

full of touch
that describe another sun
and all the dark
fractured in between

stillness sings
the grace of geometry
the shattered symmetry
the silk of the circuitry

scribed into the sky
that separates
us

sea glass

I let the sea
hold my brokenness
run it's tongue
over my jagged edges
let it sing my serrations
down to smoke
turn me opaque
a stone petal

now ready
to be placed in your hand
listen to the cuts
in your skin

is that how we heal
to be touched gently
again and again
and again

is love the waves
we walk into

each step
blunts our blades
shatters our rage
the little lashes
that scar us smooth

grinds down the incisors
of our hungry kisses
till we are just
a fragment of tongue

etched through with light
tasting the soot
of shadows
pooled in palms

glad

I had these days with you
blossom
falling through us
sunlight
touching us
at the same time
the tide
sipping from our footsteps

give you

the flickering filaments
from faraway fields
blesses from blossom
calmness of cobbles
stroked by sun
the sun's pelt
still attached to the dark pinprick
of its heart
the sigh of shadows
creeping in and out of corners
the silence
brimming within bells
the wishes
weeping from wells
spindrift of stars
dusting silent streets
the blackness from blackberries
the moon's melody
plumes of pillows
fire from feathers
fur from my furnace
cries from my candle
smoke from silver
the ghost of gold

holding hands

between our palms
create a thimble
of darkness
swing it between us
a censer
ribbons of smoke
seep from between
our weaved fingers
vapour trails
fade as they fall
tatters behind us
treetops tap fingertips
above

crisscross our paths
folded into each other's hands

two frozen lakes
etched by the blades of skaters

face to face
licking each other's scratched calligraphy

the sparks from our tails
the trace of our tears

preserved in the dark
between palms

weight

air heavy
with hope not given
sky pressing everything
a fraction deeper
into the fields
wish I could give you all this
the shadows not stretching
but seeping
out of the hedgerows
the stillness
of abandoned farm machinery
that's already begun
its slow bloom of rust
just by being still
the way crows seem to birth
wet and slick
from the gape of its wounds
grace of power lines
that fracture the sky
like it dropped itself
broke where it was meant to break
split along its songlines
their gentle cambers
part of what I want to give
along with all the weight
of all the songbirds
that rested for handfuls of seconds
and all those seconds
crushed to hours
wish I could give
the way dusk does
everything all at once

to everyone who needs it
which is everyone
but most of all
wish I could give all this
old sunlight and stillness
to you
you who bruised me
with the gentle taps of sunlight
held in your fingertips
blood coaxed to surface
darkness sung from the seabed
who gave me a dead arm
with the gentle blush of blonde
bruised me all over
all at once
you wouldn't have known
the damage done
as for a second I flared
a notch brighter
it will take years
a lifetime
for this full body haemorrhage
to fully develop
even my blood will bruise
cut open my corpse
I will soak you with storms
cry crows
burst songbirds
jump start the sky
gift you
all the ungiven hope

standing in front of the sun

followed the brushstrokes of smoke
led me to your dawn
and dusk soaked fields

saw you
the ghost of a silhouette
in front of the sun

skin thinned transparent
saw monsterful mirages in the quiver
of your flammable thoughts

saw the slow blooms
from the soft detonations
of your heartbeat
saw your torn edges flare

saw the blackberry
currents of your blood
river the length of you

saw the lace of your lungs
pulse like filaments
as they filtered light from the air

blown through me
felt your ash still glowing
blossom burrowed into my mind

saw the smoke of your songs
lining your throat
saw the tinder box
of your voice box

saw your eyes
and somehow
because they were darker
they were brighter

gloaming walk

treetops touch fingertips
above our walk
through this kingdom of dusk
shadows coalesce to a wren
in the hollow made
by our held hands
size of a womb
shape of a flame
sigh-swings between us
song trickles from the seams
fingers turn to flints
spilling sparks
into our shadows
stretching behind us

promise

if we
do not meet in this life
promise we'll meet
in another field
where rust dusts
the faces of flowers
where bees brew oil
sun flares shadows
and shadows burn bright
stretch across streets

from there
promise we'll walk
beyond fields that sigh
where choir
claws the sky
and evensong
threads as smoke
through diminished winds

where moths
flames for wings
line sooty walls
of blown hearts
feed on turpentine
that weeps from the scars
it seals

phantom paths

drizzle reveals cobwebs
chimed by the stillness
ghosts of breaths
settled to the sides of steps
beneath stairs
that leads to the garden
where the sibilance
of your skirt
stroked the grass
that whispers your faded
footsteps

scars remember
kisses of the blade
shadows remember
what it was like
to pool in the shallows
printed in the shore
by our soles

drizzle
dust from a dream

the trickle of a path
towards a tree

made by ghosts
tore their fabric

on the shadows
of its leaves

wish we walked fields together
before we knew
walking the fields
was all that mattered

brushed by the hem of the late suns skirt
footprints brim silver

smoke the paths
revealed by the loss of light

our ghosts
deepen the desire
keep the paths burning

our silent songlines
wait for our voices
to surface again

wind walks the grass
sings the streets
between us

goes on ahead
feels its way
with its faint fingertips

wind takes a rubbing of the sky
its charcoal fingers
reveals its grain

the sky's tender scratches
its touch describes the darkness
of not holding you

wind slips up my sleeves
flares between my shirt and skin

wind licks the wounds
it gave itself

sky shivered
deep space distorted

fingers damp with kisses
pinch out our guttering flames

let the river unravel us
back to threads

riddle it with smoke
ghost bright

let's walk those walks
beside an even darker river

same sun
touches us
at the same time

our silver song
sung soft
as newborn soles

Andrew Martin currently lives and works in Devon, UK. He studied wildlife illustration in Carmarthen, South Wales, which has imbued his writing and artwork with elemental and natural world imagery. For him, writing poetry follows the same creative process he uses in the generation of his digital artwork.

He has had highly commended poems in both the Bridport Prize and the Hippocrates Prize and was shortlisted for the first Venture Award for a poetry pamphlet. He also runs Shoals of Starlings Press, has appeared on BBC and local Radio, and pens the popular poetry blog shoalsofstarlings.com

Other books:
Shoals of Starlings (2020)
Solar Satellites (2020)

Love and gratitude
to a shard of slate,
a woolly mammoth,
a dead bear
and a toad.

www.ingramcontent.com/pod-product-compliance
Lightning Source LLC
Chambersburg PA
CBHW022124040426
42450CB00006B/840